ℋℋℬ

Bring Me
Her
Heart

Poems by

Sarah Getty

Higganum Hill Books : Higganum, Connecticut

First Edition
First Printing, May 1, 2006

Higganum Hill Books
P. O. Box 666, Higganum, CT. 06441-0666
Ph: (860) 345-4103
Email: rcdebold@mindspring.com

ISBN10: 0-9741158-8-6
ISBN13: 978-0-9741158-8-6
Library of Congress Control Number: 2005023805

Edited by Arthur S. Wensinger, Wesleyan University.

Cover: *The Wicked Queen*, Ludwig Grimm. From *Schneewittchen (Snow White)*, *Märchen für Kinderhände*, 1825.

Library of Congress Cataloging-in-Publication Data

Getty, Sarah, 1943-
  Bring me her heart : poems / by Sarah Getty.-- 1st ed.
    p. cm.
  ISBN-13: 978-0-9741158-8-6 (alk. paper)
  ISBN-10: 0-9741158-8-6 (alk. paper)
  I. Title.
  PS3557.E885B75 2006
  811'.54--dc22
                          2005023805

Independent Publishers Group distributes Higganum Hill Books.
Ph: (800) 888-4741   www.ipgbook.com or www.calliope.org/hhb/

Printed in the United States of America.

iv

Dedication

Again, for David, who makes it possible.

In memory of my Mother, Davina Graham Ely Sovereign

and

my father, John Howard Sovereign.

ACKNOWLEDGMENTS

Some of these poems have been published previously, as follows:

"The Black Sea," *Paris Review* 167, Fall, 2003

"Down in the Dark," *Western Humanities Review* LIII, No.3, Fall 1999

"The Earth Is Saying," *Paris Review* 153, Winter 1999-2000

"Edens," *Paris Review* 167, Fall, 2003

"Galatea to the Unborn Paphos," *Western Humanities Review* LV, 2, Fall 2001

"Gepetto in the Belly of the Dogfish," *Western Humanities Review* LIII, 1, Spring 1999

"Lewis Carroll's Last Photograph of Alice Liddell," *Massachusetts Review* XLII, Spring, 2001

"On Wingaersheek Beach," *Western Humanities Review* LII, 2, Summer 1998

"3:00 A.M: Questioning Cassiopeia," *Western Humanities Review* LII, 3, Fall 1998

"To Speak With the Dead," *Paris Review* 173, Spring 2005

"Late Day," *The Eleventh Muse,* 2005

"In October" *Fourth River I,* 2005

"Certain Maples" *Fourth River* I, 2005

"Nesting Dolls," *Diner V, 1, Spring/Summer, 2005*

"Who Was That Masked Man?" *Calyx,* forthcoming.

Grateful acknowledgement is made to:

Peter T. Struck and the University of Pennsylvania for permission to use information and quoted text in "Eleusis."

G.E. Mylonas and Princeton University Press for permission to use quoted text from Pindar's *Odes* in "Eleusis" and change "he" to "she."

The Ecole Initiative, Evansville College, for information on the Eleusinian mysteries.

The Loeb Classical Library for the Hugh G. Evelyn-White translation of "The Homeric Hymn to Demeter," adapted and quoted in "Eleusis."

Little Brown for Emily Dickinson's "I've never seen a moor," quoted in "Procession."

MacMillan Publishers for William Butler Yeats' "The Lake Isle of Innisfree," quoted in

"Procession."

Oxford University Press for Samuel Taylor Coleridge's "Kubla Khan," quoted in "Obituary."

Poems quoted in "Chant and Dance" were originally published by MacMillan Publishers, Charles Scribner's Sons, the Poetry Bookshop, and Harper and Brothers.

Silver Pennies, originally published in 1922 by MacMillan, was reissued by Buccaneer Book in 1976.

"Trio from an Imaginary Opera" contains two brief quotations from Mary Shelley's *Frankenstein, or the Modern Prometheus,* Lackington, Hughes, Harding, Mavor and Jones, 1818.

"Thesaurus" is freely adapted from Peter Mark Roget's Introduction to his *Thesaurus,* 1852.

With special thanks to Moira Linehan.

CONTENTS

2. Things Revealed

3. Things Said

4. Late Day

1

*THOSE WHO STRUGGLE
WITH THE DIFFICULTIES
OF COMPOSITION*

THE UNVEILING OF TRUTH
Sargent, sketch for a mural

If Truth sat on a chair, not
the ground. If the drape revealed
more than the bumps of brow, nose,

breast and knee. If that gesture —
hands head-high and still under
the veil, ready to throw back

the black-on-white charcoaled folds —
were not so like our nightmares
of the sheeted dead, rising.

If she looked less like she might flap
and fly, albino vampiress,
half-blind in this dim room's light.

If Salome had not danced.
If Truth were not a woman.

If we knew nothing of cauls.

THE EARTH IS SAYING

Roots and rocks emerge from the forest path like half-spoken thoughts,
or as Thoreau would put it, the earth is saying "rock." And saying "root,"
too, and tiny bright red mushrooms and green moss worn smooth like a poem
one's fingered for years. Bedraggled cat-tails, a few yellow, early-fallen
leaves, but summer lingers – the scented air is warm and spangled with sun-
lit motes. Roots make earthen steps, but here, where my favorite tree
stands like the pine in a Japanese poem, roots multiply, so that I need

to walk with care on the uneven earth. But I need to get near this tree, I need
it for a poem, recycled from the Japanese. As I walk, I need my thoughts
to take in the rocks and roots, those thoughts still half-spoken by the earth.
But this is silly – I am old enough to know that neither the earth nor the sun
thinks, or cares what I think, or needs to be put in a poem. Nor does a tree.
It is presumption to think this, or think that to be old, and to walk in the fall
woods and say that the earth is uttering rocks is all right, because one is a poet.

Nor will it do to think about one's age in the fall woods, or write poems
about leaves turning, hair and seasons turning, etc. There is no need
for a poem like that – it has been done already by plenty of other poets.
Even the pine, looking so Japanese here by the pond where yellow leaves fall
and float and lily pads like green plates serve up their white blooms – this tree,
so poetic, has no wish to be recycled into something that is only a thought
and not a living thing rooted in the earth while all its needles shine in the sun.

So, like the woodman in the old poem, I'll spare that tree and let the sun-
shine fall wordless on the still pond and the golden needles fallen on the earth.
I'll walk without thinking and just look at the roots as they spring from the earth
and the rocks that crop up over eons like stubborn, monotonous thoughts.
Re-cycling is for cans and jars. I'll let the woods surround my thoughts,

4

but not enter them. I'll pocket no leaf or red mushroom to prompt my need
to write poems, although it's a true proverb: "There's nothing new under the sun,"

and poets have long walked in the yellow woods and felt how the fall sun
was warm, but not quite like summer, and seen leaves falling and had a thought
or two about getting old and how everything recycles. And if I need to root
around and find a tree for a poem, who's to say "no"? The earth? The rocks?

GEPETTO IN THE BELLY OF THE DOGFISH
to Carlo Collodi 1826 - 1890

In my little house, a hearth fire burned day and night,
boiling a steaming pot. It was paint,
merely, daubed onto the wall,
but served after sunset to support
my spirits. So even in here, I've made a little

house, with table, chair, and cupboard from your ship. And you,
Miss Figurehead, propped, bowsprit and all,
across the table from me
to listen, and nod, and smile as I
require — as I imagine it. For I am not mad;

I know that you are wooden, merely. Who, if not I,
could see how the knife-strokes freed your face
and figure from the wood? Good
hands he had, your maker, a gift from
the gods, who once had power to turn us into trees.

Reversing that trick is given to a few, who feel
the human form emerge from the wood
as Apollo felt Daphne's
vanish beneath his hands. Yes, that old
story I've told you how many times in these two years?

And there was one about a man who carved a woman
of ivory, so perfect he fell
in love. He dressed her in silks
and trinkets and kept her in his bed!
Venus, goddess of such things, took pity on the fool

and made her live. Rubbish! Pinocchio moved his eyes
while my knife was finishing the lids.
He spoke with wooden lips, stuck
out his tongue, when all the rest of him
was still a log. As soon as I shaped the legs, they kicked!

They ran away! He was wicked, but he was alive!
Alive, and made of wood, my Pinecone
Head! I thought that log would make
a money-making puppet – but greed
can't bring wood to life. Inside me, like the form that hides

in the tree, a longing was alive. And thus I got
my son, the way that Greek got his wife,
senza the meddling goddess.
So you'll forgive, my dear, my giving
you no silks, no kisses. It's my boy I long for day

and night. That work was worthy of a Leonardo
(I say to your wooden ears alone)!
His ears were – well, I skipped them,
he did fidget so. My own fault, then,
that he never heard my warnings or curbed his folly.

But when I saw him last – in that storm, in my little
boat – he dived (I think) head-long from land's
end into the sea. I heard
his voice: "Papa, I will save you!" Brave,
foolish Wooden Head! That's why I've hung on, eating stale

ship's biscuit, breathing this fish stink. I think, too, of those
old stories, especially the ones
with wonders in them. If wood
can walk and talk — well, then, why shouldn't
the things I dream about come true? And as the story's

end gets closer (this is the last candle, and I ate
your last hard tack two days past) the chance
of unlikely happenings
increases. As it has to, you see.
So Jonah is spit out on the shore, or the monster's

head is severed, the maiden alive in its jaws, or
rescue arrives as the last candle
gutters. That girl, the Fairy
with Blue Hair — said (or did I dream it?)
that Pinocchio has promised to be good. And if

he can keep his word, she'll work a spell, she said, to make
him "a real boy." A boy made of flesh
and blood, she meant, like any
boy killing cats in any alley.
Bah! Where's the rarity in that? Let him stay as I

made him, a miracle of craft! What is flesh? A curse,
merely — this cough, these aching joints, these
rotting feet. My son, the boy
made of wood, could still be capering
a hundred, two hundred, three hundred years from today!

Alone, you say? Yes – unique, incomparable. Why should
he need a wife? I never had one!
Unless it might be you, dear
Baucis, so soon to be my widow.
You weep, as if grief itself had made this salty pool

I live in. Soon I'll lie down on the table – but not
to be eaten! To preserve myself
for a while from the whittling
of this womb. Nothing left to do now
but follow the old Romans' mode – though no story tells

of a Roman dying inside a fish! One was saved
by a dolphin, one rescued by his
son – but why are you smiling?
Ah, yes – I hear it now! A splashing!
Splash and splash, the sound of someone walking. I think – yes!

I *know* those footsteps! I made those feet! Oh, is hunger
making me its fool? Is this hope all
imagination, merely?
Or can the impossible ending
end the tale? Splash and splash...let me hold up the candle...

Pen and ink, 10 1/2 x 8 inches,
RL 19097v

A man with angelic locks and a woman
with no head are sketched *in flagrante*, standing
up. Or rather, *he* stands, while she levitates

at a convenient height, not having a leg
to stand on. They are hemisected not side-
to-side, like Aristophanes' poor human

halves, but (as Plato has him put it) "Verti-
cally, down their noses, like people in profile
on their tombstones." Except for the penis — that

pumped-up appendage is shown intact, loving-
ly rounded, made real by skilled strokes of shading.
But nevertheless, transparent. We can see

that a duct runs from the spine to the penis,
and, paralleling the urethra, issues
at an upper aperture. This channel, as

Avicenna tells us, draws the "animal
spirit" from the spinal cord to do its work
in procreation. But since the heart is seat

of the emotions, another duct connects
that organ to the testes, which are "the source
of ardor." And on the distaff side, we find

a tube from uterus to nipple – the blood
retained in pregnancy being turned to milk.
But this is wrong! Not geniuses, or artists,

or dissectors of anything since high school
frogs, we know a thing or two in this regard.
Aha! The text says that this early drawing

(1492-93) displays,
in extreme, the younger Leonardo's bent
for "creating fictitious forms to fulfill

speculative functions." Unschooled in the Re-
naissance, he read the old lore and drew what those
authorities wrote. Only later, as news

of a land denied by and denying maps
spread (along with syphilis) through Italy,
did he begin to see things for himself. Hands-

on and in up to the elbows, he groped through
fat and muscle to seize the real article –
ovaries, testicles, heart. He started it.

And we new worldlings, empirical, informed
up to our eyebrows, with five hundred more years
spent observing our own and one another's

bodies.... Well, we carry on. Poor human halves,
groping, coupling, rebounding like bumper cars.
By George, we still don't get it – we've only learned

that there's no connection to the heart. We read
the authorities, Web-chat with Dr. Ruth.
To keep the machine in shape, we sweat, and eat

like birds. We hop about hapless and hopeful
as the Half Chick, creating fictitious forms
to fulfill speculative functions. There's no

science in this experimental method.
Best, then, to think of it as art — sketches, first
drafts, a series of cartoons. "Who knows?" we tell

ourselves, "out there, off the map, a great, perfect
something may come of this one day — a Mona
Lisa, a Jesus, a profile for my tomb."

EDENS

Like God, I get up early, walk out in the cool of the day
to see my handiwork. Oh, Nathaniel, thou hast not done well!
I'll post a sign: *Henry Thoreau, poet and pencil-maker,*
who planted this garden as a wedding gift for Nathaniel
Hawthorne and his bride, does by this notice publicly foreswear

responsibility for its present deplorable state.
Pigweed in the parsnips, the radishes choked with grass — alas,
my friend, how you have lapsed! "Paradise" you call it, say you live
here like Adam and Eve. Husbandry! The garden must give place
to the bedchamber this marriage month! The window of that shrine

looks out this way, but I think your handsome head will not appear,
framed in its panes like a portrait drawn and quartered. No, finer
sights than my ungainly frame will delight your eye this morning!
I'll pull up a few weeds for good nature's sake — when Adam delved,
he was a bachelor, I'll wager. And worked on the Sabbath,

like a savage. There — the row of Bull's Blood beet is free and clear,
still straight as the day I eyed the line and dropped the seed. Cuckoo-
like, I leave my offspring here — and there, too, within my neighbor
Waldo's gates. Yet I'm a poor sort of rogue, a local rover,
returning to cluck and fuss. There's the church bell — inside the house,

perhaps, you rise and put on Sunday best. But no — you're pagans
now, like me. "Apollo," she calls you. Then I'm no father-God,
but Vulcan, shaped to labor while Phoebus takes his ease. Helpmeet
have I none, nor have I need for Eve or Venus, fashioned
of bone or clay. Here's Purple Dragon carrot I chose to mock

13

your flights of fancy, and the tomato called King Umberto,
hero of an Italianate romance. You write for women —
magic mantles, elixirs of youth, vaporous whatnots glimpsed
in twilight, torchlight, mist. Fairy tales! Moonshine! I'm too plain
a fellow for such stuff. With dirty hands, like Virgil, I'll write

my rural verses, rooted in the real. What thing more wondrous
can you conceive than seed becoming vine? Give me soil and rain
and I'll exchange flesh for foliage, tap down to granite and take
my radical grip. I'll be a pole bean plant, feeding the babes
of Adam and his mate. Your purse, it's whispered, lacks the magic

to make coins come again. Ousted from your Paradise, eastward
in Salem you'll sweat to earn your bread. Go with my blessing — found
a new race there, exiled but innocent. Fiction moves forward,
poetry twines. Here in Concord, where the climate suits, I'll build
a garden shed shelter, live alone on poetry and beans.

LEWIS CARROLL'S LAST PHOTOGRAPH OF ALICE LIDDELL

It will end with my going out like a candle. *Then*
you can do what you like – spend my last
cent like a madman, marry,
if you must – but not that low
creature you say you love, a scheming,
faithless widow who flouts her vows. She *has* a husband,

killed in the war that took your brothers. Yes, one must mourn,
forever. Why should I not follow
the late Queen's example? See,
in this picture: I started
at eighteen (or eleven, when we
became...strangers). No, I was sad! Well, sulking a bit,

too. It was years since I'd been to his rooms; why Mama
said yes, I can't think. Except – the books
had made him a famous man
by then, and she *was* a snob.
She came along, of course, and watched him
like a hawk. You had to hold still so long; it took me

back to all those times I'd sat there, dressed like a beggar
maid or Chinese lady. Or I'd lie
down "asleep," an easier
pose to hold. And while I held
still, my head would fill up with pictures –
our trips on the river with my sisters, the picnics,

the stories, the magic tricks he did. Yes, it was he
who taught me that sleight-of-hand you boys
liked so when you were little.
Why *should* I have mentioned it?
We never spoke of him — as good as dead,
and when he did die, Mama made sure not a Liddell

was seen at his funeral. He was odd, to be sure,
but people are, it's only the style
that changes. Now it's savage
jazz and motor cars and mad
dancing. Flapper widows! Don't try me,
Caryl, with that nonsense. The Reverend Mr.

Dodgson (he was a Deacon, you know) had dignity
the Scots Guards never taught you. He looked
like he'd swallowed a poker,
Papa said. Oh, he was strict!
He wouldn't stand blaspheming, he'd freeze
any boy who let slip an impure word. Discretion,

self-control — you might recall those virtues your father
and I used to mention? Old-fashioned
as you please, but *there* was free-
dom for you! I was a Queen
in his rooms, it was a different world.
There were costumes, cabinets of magical toys — oh!

I can't tell you — I had such powers, as if my feet
could float above the floor! There were rules,
but not the ones Mama made.
The way you felt when you played
in the sea — remember? or running
about naked after your bath? (My own three cherubs!

and you the only one left to me!) No, no, you won't
find me in *those* pictures, not in one!
Little girls with no clothes on —
why, Mama would have had Miss
Prickett's head! Our governess that was;
she went with us to his rooms, and all of Oxford talked.

The poor thing had her hopes, but I knew I had his heart.
In my mind, we were married — little
girls make their plans, they're schemers
by instinct. And they sense things —
his suffering, his love — I *knew* them,
like a story from the Bible. Oh, my yes, we read

the Bible with him, had lessons in logic and chess.
He would have made us into — angels,
I suppose, was what he longed
for. And I was an angel!
See — here I am, haloed with roses.
It was like Eden, right on Tom Quad, until Mama

put a stop to it. I should have asked her why before
she died. Years later, they said he'd asked
her for my hand. So – *that* can
shock you? Back then, it happened.
But Mama would never have settled
for a stammering minor don. No, there was nothing

he did – well, those pictures of other girls....The point is,
I was never in his rooms again
until that day. You see now
why I was sad? And it seems
to me that I could see, as I sat,
how the years to come would prove that no happiness can

last. Even kissing a Prince! He was the youngest son,
godfather to your brother Leo –
but that story has bored you
for ages. We danced all night
at his graduation ball. My gown
was palest rose, it seemed we were waltzing upon clouds....

He loved me! But his mother put a stop to it. (None
of Mr. Dodgson's stories ended
with a wedding and a Prince.)
The Queen must have a Princess,
so off with my head! And at the same
time I lost my little sister, Edith. Here she is,

with me and Lorina, pretending to play guitars.
The three of us would sing together
so prettily — how I wish
you could have heard! She never
wore her pale pink gown, she lay in pain
while I was at the ball. Peritonitis — in one

week she was gone. It was then I understood — while *he*
had sorrow, I could have no gladness,
for I was his invention.
I was old when I married
your father, almost thirty. I made
our life a country paradise —
ponies and roses,

puppies and croquet. I had learned well how to manage
things from living under Mama's rule.
I think you boys were happy —
any childhood is magic,
if there is kindness, and order.   But
I couldn't weave the spell as he did — I never paid

the price. And even if I had, it would have ended —
it is a Vale of Tears we live in, though
you and your widow deny
it with both hands. Tweedle-Dee
and Tweedle Dum resolved to have
a battle, and my sons were dead. I'm to blame, I know,

for making you a spoiled, willful boy.   Yes, you *are*
my boy, though you bellow "forty-two"
at me. I can't put a stop
to your folly – the world's gone
mad now, and mothers have shrunk to pawns.
But I will not bless your marriage to that slut! Don't raise

your hand to me – I was married in the Abbey, grand
as a Queen. The Prince named his daughter
after me – I am Alice,
famous right around the world!
Oh, my dear boy, if we could just be
peaceful for a day together, I would say these things

better, I would curtsey and turn out my toes! *He* said
that when we die, we will find ourselves
among the bright flowerbeds
and cool fountains, and all those
we have lost will be there. I'll see *him*
again, and Edith, and Leo and Alan and your

father. A woman can't have two husbands, don't you see?
It would be awkward! (And *he* would not
be pleased.) Oh, Caryl, one must
be as a child to enter
that little door! Be a good boy, do –
hold Mama's hand, and together we'll look for the key!

PORTRAIT OF THE ARTIST

*Slumber, 1993: Performance with loom, yarn, bed, nightgown, EEG machine and artist's REM
reading*
  — Massachusetts Museum of Contemporary Art

I. The Scene

We see here not the performance, but
the set-up: furniture, of a sort, arranged
          in a wood-beamed room
          of this old brick mill.
The artist, who might make sense of it, has gone,
leaving, stage right, a rack of spindles,
          a bed dead center,
          and, stage left, a loom.
Forty threads rise from the rack and pass
through the air for twenty feet before they reach
          the loom. Under them
          is the bed—the threads
traverse it head to foot, suggesting, perhaps,
a canopy. The loom takes them in,
          rolls them out again
          as whole cloth that drops
to the floor, piles up, unfolds, stretches
out straight as a sidewalk leading to the bed,
          where it climbs the foot
          creeps to the pillow —
is a blanket! And there's a pattern in it,
peaks and valleys picked out in colored
          strips. The same jagged
          lines scroll out in ink

from the EEG machine back there,
by the wall. A sign says: *The artist, during*
her performance, weaves
the blanket all day
and sleeps on the bed, under the blanket, at night.
The machine records her rapid eye
movements (REM), plotting
a graph of her dreams.
When she wakes up, she weaves the REM graph's
pattern into the blanket, using strips ripped
from her nightgown, made
from cloth printed here
in this mill when it housed the Arnold Print Works.

II.   The Dream

The green calico
rips clean, nightie now
up to my knees. I weave the sprigged print
in, out, above, below the threads. Why do my
fingers seem asleep?
My breath goes in, out,
in, out, hasty, pained. I must finish, finish
before it's too late. Too late! I hear
their voices weaving
on the stairs. And wrong!
It's all wrong! My fingers hook the strip,
tear the green bargellos from the warp. Useless!
I must start again.
Bright girls' voices, blue,

red, green: *You ask her! I asked her last time. You*
ask her! She never answers, silly!

They spill through the door

and stand in a herd,

nervous, not coming near. That one holds
her little sister by the hand. They whisper:

It's too old-fashioned,

that loom; she's wasting

time. *Why's she keep tearing her nightgown? Showing*
her legs like a slut. I know that green

stuff — wove it last spring!

I saw her sleeping,

once. *She'd things like curlers on her head,*
with threads coming out that went to that machine.

You never! I did!

See how it's got lights?

Electricity! Alice, don't go near there!
And the machine was drawing something

all by itself! See

that paper down there

by her feet? It's what she's weaving, ain't
it? Don't say ain't, it isn't educated.

Ugly, isn't it?

Shush! You'll make her cry!

Even that little girl knows my work's no good!
I lift my nightie to wipe my tears.

Ooh, don't look, Maisy!

Why, she has no shame!

If only they'd stop talking and look,
really look, I think they'd understand. I point

at the bed, the cloth.

I point with both hands

23

at the pattern – can't they see? *Looks like mountains,*
don't – doesn't it? Maybe she's homesick –
>   *You from New Hampshire,*
>   *Miss? She won't tell us,*
you know she won't ever talk. Maybe
she can't talk, maybe she's a dummy. Maybe
>   *she's put away here,*
>   *you know, crazy-like.*
Giggles. Edging toward the stairs. But they don't leave –
I amuse them. If I could only
>   do this right, they'd see
>   what my weaving means,
and why I stay here – sweating, hectic,
longing to wander where the river water
>   braids its blue and white
>   around the gray rocks.
There's such – I mean – it's – I have to show them! *How'd*
she get here? You ever seen her eat?
>   *Has she no home? No*
>   *sense? Has she no work?*

THESAURUS: A Partially Found Poem

Completion, n.
Finish, termination, conclusion, end of the matter

There is, of course, no end when the matter is the great riches
in which the *alma mater* — English, our mother tongue — abounds.
But my book, at last, is done, and I give thanks to Him whose word
made light that I have lived to see this day. Seventy-one years
old and due, no doubt, for termination, I will leave the world
this treasure house, that those who struggle with the difficulties

of composition shall no longer strive ineffectually
to devise forms of expression which shall faithfully portray
their thoughts and sentiments. To these, my Work holds out a helping
hand. Dictionaries put meanings to the word you have in mind —
my book puts words to meanings. The idea, you see, comes first:
I have sorted all possible ideas into their classes

and relations. This is the basis of my categories
of words, which are but the symbols of ideas. With my book,
the inquirer can readily select, out of the ample
collection spread out before his eyes, those expressions most fit
to express his thought. By this means he may avoid that painful
groping that leads to clumsy paraphrase or to tortuous

circumlocution.

Class, n.

Classification, categorization, arrangement, taxonomy

I am a doctor and man of Science, that fair Handmaid
to the progress of Mankind. You may have seen my articles
on insects, electricity, optics, and the like — all based
upon my own experiments. Too, a logarithmic scale
of my invention has produced a sliding rule that's proven
useful. At length, like Leibnitz, I have applied my mind to language:

my verbal classes follow the principle that is employed
in the study of Natural History. Thus, the sectional
divisions correspond to the natural families found
in Botany and Zoology, and the relationship
of words forms a network analogous to the natural
filiation of plants or animals. My system lays out

in six classes the ideas which are expressible in words —
to wit, ABSTRACT RELATIONSHIPS, SPACE, the MATERIAL WORLD,
INTELLECT, VOLITION, and our SENTIENT and MORAL POWERS.
The words and phrases that convey ideas in each of these six
classes are arranged, within my book, under one thousand Head
Words displayed in two parallel columns to illustrate

opposite and correlative ideas. Thus, a writer
wishing to speak of love would turn to Class Six, Division Two:
Interpersonal Emotion, Head Word 887.
(See page xix, Tabular Synopsis of Categories.)
I have of course omitted terms for items not connected
with general ideas, such as objects in natural

history. Exceptions must, however, be made in favour
of such words as admit of metaphorical application
to general subjects. Thus, the word *Lion* will find a place
under the heading *Courage; Anchor*, being emblematic
of *Hope*, appears among the words expressing that emotion,
and in like manner, *butterfly* and *weathercock*, suggestive

of fickleness, are both included in the category
of irresolution. Bear in mind, I pray, that in this work
I do not attempt to clarify the significations
of words, but rather to sort them according to the senses
in which they now are used. Nor do I presume to enter here
upon the task of distinguishing between words apparently

synonymous.

Order, n.
Uniformity, regularity, judgment, precept, command

It is not my intention to regulate the use of words,
but simply to provide a range of tools, leaving the choice
to the discretion of the employer. That said, I must own
it has occurred to me that my work could help to establish
a clear, authoritative standard which might tend to limit
those fluctuations to which language has always been subject.

Some writers indulge in the arbitrary fabrication
of new words and new-fangled phraseology. This vicious
practice, the offspring of indolence or conceit, must imply
an ignorance of legitimated words that would convey
precisely the same meaning as those they so recklessly coin
in the illegal mint of their own fancy.   It is my view

that what is needed in this age of turmoil and too-rapid
change is not originality, but clearness, discipline,
and a regard for custom. Let each man know his thought and choose
his words with care, aided by a perusal of these pages.
Let each who hears employ a like exactness. Let Speech, at last,
become a Science — let my Work quell confusion and vanquish

ambiguity!

Prophesy, v.
Foresee, predict, divine, forecast, warn

And to this end, I pray that one who comes after me shall make
a greater work, with words for each idea laid out in columns:
English, French, German, Italian, a *Polyglot Lexicon*
to assist the translator and be the means of accurate
comparison of languages, their merits and their defects.
Such analysis alone can determine the principles

on which a strictly Philosophical language might be built.
Once adopted by every civilized nation, this new tongue
will fulfill that splendid aspiration of philanthropists —
the establishment of a Universal Language. Nothing,
I believe, would more conduce to bring about a golden age
of unity and concord among the several nations

and races of mankind than the removal of that bar
to mutual understanding interposed by differences
of language. That higher civilization to which the world
is tending will see, I trust, a new and bolder effort crowned
with success. This goal, of such vast utility, should not meet
with greater hardships than other projects which in former times

appeared unfeasible yet were achieved by persevering
exertions of the human intellect. The Rosetta Stone
unriddles the Sphinx's glyphs; unlettered masons wrote the great
book of Chartres. Ambition! That alone lifts men above their state!
With my Work as bricks for building, may that tower rise!   May God
say again, relenting, "They are one people and their language

one."

2

THAT OLD STORY

TO SPEAK WITH THE DEAD
for Moira Linehan

First, go to Hell — I mean, seek out the Halls
                of Hades and his consort,
Persephone the Dread. Here's what you'll need:
                foodstuffs, a boat with sails,
vessels of water, wine, etc.
                (see libations list below),
a young ram, a black ewe, and — don't forget —
                a sword. Then conjure a wind

to blow you clear across River Ocean.
                When you see Persephone's
Grove, draw up your boat and drive your livestock
                inland. Find the spot — it's marked
by a dark peak of rock — where the River
                of Flaming Fire and the River
of Wailing (you'll know it) flow together
                into Acheron. There, use

the sword to dig a trench a cubit square
                and sprinkle the libations
around it in this order: milk and honey,
                sweetened wine, water, and white
barley.   Call aloud upon the spirits
                of the dead. Next, slit the throats
of the young ram and the black ewe, holding
                their heads down towards Erebus

while you turn your own aside.   Let their blood
            fill the trench.   Then flay and burn
the bodies while you pray – first to all
            the gods, then to Great Hades
and Wise Persephone   But keep your sword
            bare in your hand as the crowd
of ghosts flutters forward, dying to drink
            the blood. Hold them off until

you spot the one you seek.   Let that one drink –
            he will grow more distinct
to your eye and gain the power of speech.
            While all the others gibber,
the shade you love will talk as sensibly
            as any living person
and answer all you ask.   But keep this rule
            in mind – you stay on your side

of the trench, the ghost on his. The two realms –
            dead, and living – must remain
apart forever, or the whole deal's off.
            No doubt you'll want to stretch out
a hand and touch that cherished face, or take
            into your arms the one form
in all the world you weep for night and day –
            But don't! You'll grasp only air;

your love will fade like dream erased by day,
        and Grief set its teeth more deeply
in your heart. That's all I can tell you.
      No one has found instructions
to help the traveler with the hardest part:
        to return to the light and live,
your ship provisioned, until Hades grants
        you leave, at long last, to sail.

CONSERVATION OF FROGS

Lucinda, dear, don't touch that nasty old frog!
Yes, the oldest in the world, the King
of the Frogs. No, he's not kin
to our King — my husband and your father —
though it's true your Father was in a frog's form

for a time, and my kiss did change him. Sit here
by me, on the well's edge, and I'll tell
you — it's time you knew. When girls
are your age, as I was then, they think
day and night about men. Don't blush — it's the way

we were made. I was sitting right here, tossing
and catching my golden ball — you know
the tale — and dreaming, of course,
of a Prince. Splash! the ball's in the well.
I sat there crying as it sank out of reach

(but slowly — it was a hollow sphere) and then —
a deep voice: "What's the matter with you,
King's daughter? Your weeping would
touch the heart of a stone." I looked up,
and — here's the part no one knows — there stood a Prince!

A handsome six-footer who fetched out my ball
just like that! He dried my tears, he put
his wet arm around my waist,
he kissed my cheek. Well, I was grateful,
so I kissed him back. Then he started doing

those things I've told you of, things allowed only
in the marriage bed. Under his green
tights I saw something jumping,
so I turned him into a frog. Oh,
my yes, I can do such things, all the women

in our family can. I'd turn the dogs into
cats — they're so much nicer — and one time
I lost my temper and changed
an insolent servant to a squirrel.
You haven't tried it yet? Well, do — but take care,

and heed my story! That night the Frog-Prince came
to dinner, like the statue in *Don
Giovanni.* I had promised,
he said, to let him eat from my plate,
drink from my cup, and sleep that night beside me

on my pillow. All this I had vowed to give,
so went his story, if only he'd
rescue my toy. I had made
no such promise! But if I denied
his lies, I knew he'd tell the truth and blame me

for his state. The golden ball sat like judgment
on my lap — my Father ordered me
to keep my word. So Froggy
ate, he drank (ugh!) from my silver cup.
I thought that would be enough, but my Father

forced me to take him to my bed. (I never
liked the way my Father touched me, kissed
me). The minute I had closed
the door, the frog was begging, "Change me
back! I'll behave! You won't be sorry." It pained

me a bit to explain: I could only do
one-way changes. "See?" I said, pointing
to Fido, the cat who lay
on my bed and watched him with switching
tail. "Still a cat, and glad of it." "Then kiss me,

he croaked. "I've heard that sometimes works." He was up-
set, I could tell. "No," I said, "I don't
want to, you're a frog." "Whose fault
is that?" he whined, but a Princess must
be choosy, as I've told you. I changed for bed,

and he hopped about after me, croaking "Kiss
me, kiss me!" until I had to stun
him with a pillow. I piled
the sofa cushions on top, wishing
for the twenty-four stacked up in that other

story. I fell asleep, letting the cat keep
watch. But he got out somehow, crept past
the cat, hopped to my pillow
and put his damp mouth on mine! I woke
up to warm lips, a Prince's kiss. Delight

undid me – my limbs were lax, and he was – well,
never mind! We were married next day,
of course, though my poor Mother
was distracted and my Father – gone!
Gone where? Oh, he's not far away, Lucinda,

though no one has seen him since that night. My Prince
asleep, I crept into my Father's
room. He snored on while I – just
some words, a pass of the hand, and then –
Don't touch, dear! Here, you can poke him with this stick.

BRING ME HER HEART

After the wedding: rice, flights of doves, and dwarves in white
satin. A 60-piece orchestra.
Snow White dances with her Prince,
the waltz almost drowning out the screams
from the dungeon where the witch is dancing in red-hot

iron shoes. The Princess hears the screams and smiles. Revenge
is the ending: Snow White wins, her mother
smiles down on her from heaven,
and the witch must dance in pain until
she dies. Years pass. The old King expires: long live the new

King and his Queen! They thrive: peace, huge harvests, and seven
royal babes, all boys.   Snow White, one day,
goes riding in the forest.
She meets an old crone struggling along
on crutches. She is moved. "Old mother, let me help you

to your home." She hoists the bag of bones onto her horse
and holds her tightly; rides til they reach
a hovel in the forest's
darkest heart. Inside, the beldam sinks
into a chair and rubs her rag-bound feet. The Queen lights

a fire, boils water, pours out tea, washes the dishes,
makes the bed. She finds an old rhythm
in it, like a dance. "Tell me
of your life," she bids the crone. The old
voice begins, "Once I was young, and happy as a queen.

My husband loved me. I was his second wife, the first
had died. We lived in a fine castle
not too far from here. We had
a daughter with skin as white as snow."
The Queen drops her cup. "Your own daughter, born of your flesh?"

"Oh, yes, how I suffered to bring her into the world!
But no blessing can last – she vanished
like a fairy's gift." "She died young?"
"She rode into the woods – these woods – one day,
and never rode out again. That day beauty died.

Since then, all loss: husband, riches, pride. A dried-out pod
my life, which once blossomed white, and red,
and black – oh, her curls as black
as ebony! Each day I wrap up
these ruined stumps and roam the forest, hoping she might…"

She weeps. The Queen shrinks back, as if the hag held out
a poisoned apple. Can two be one
in these woods, and evil good?
Can stories go astray? She searches
the furrowed face. Could it be that first face, that mirror

she gazed up on from the breast? And the feet – does she dare
to unwind the rags? Her heart, so long
a casket full of hate, gapes,
a velvet hollow red as blood.
The crone looks up with eyes like riddles. "What do you wish?"

"I wish…" but what to say? "Change back to my first mother,
who was kind"? Or, "Change back
to my enemy, young and fair,
against whom I built my strength"? Snow White,
lost, asks: "Do you know me? Can you tell me who I am?"

I came to life beneath him — his face, joy, and heaven
in my first sight blended. He is my maker
and mother, all that I know he taught
me. Now he says you are here
inside me — I, only four
months alive, will become a mother.
How Aphrodite gave me life he's told me,
but how you came to be is harder..... From the Goddess,

too, he says, but in another way — not by his skill
in carving, but by the love She blesses. Man
and woman, not ivory and knife,
can make a life. Or gods can,
but only where there's belief.
I believe she gave me breath, reward
for his devotion, but how can I believe
his tale of a baby that grows from a seed? My mind

is a child's, he says. I must learn from watching — how grain
has grown tall since I woke, and fruit has ripened.
That is the work of Time, which passes
unseen as the wind and leaves
a change behind. The children
I see in the marketplace, he says,
will be taller at the Goddess's next feast.
And some men, perhaps the old priest, bent as the olive

tree beside the temple door, will be dead — like the goats
he offers up to the Goddess. Not throat-cut
and bloody, but sacrificed by Time,
a wind that lays waste and takes
away the breath. After that,
he says, the old man will grow silent
and stiff as an effigy of ivory
or wood. But not fit for eyes' delight, as an artist

would carve a man — still shrunk and wrinkled as a fruit left
too long on the sill. It is the way we end,
he tells me — the black-wrapped crone who rocks
beside the fire was young once
(as if the wind blew backwards)
and fair as — not as fair as I, made
in Aphrodite's likeness, but fair as one
bred by mortal Cyprians could be. Ah — I mistake myself —

I, too, am mortal Cyprian, and will cease to breathe
and move "one distant day," he says, when the wind
has blown...has blown for a long, long Time.
This is too hard for me — child
inside me, I can believe
in your birth, for I feel you flutter
like a leaf. But that you will grow tall as I
(and as fair? for he made you, too) and become "one day"

the mother of a child, while I sit withered, rocking
by the fire – all this is just a tale to me.
There is a gift vouchsafed to mortals
that I do not have – that knack
of seeing what's not yet true.
Could she not give me life and that gift
too? Perhaps She judged his faith enough for both
a man and the wife he got in answer to his prayers.

He's tried to teach me – it's making pictures in the mind,
as if I drew myself and you, my baby,
sleeping in my arms, and wrote "next year"
beneath it. "Next year" will come
when Time has brought the harvest
and the cold winter he tells me of
and spring begins again. And so year after
year, as Time blows by, you'll grow, and we will grow older.

Oh, that's the hardest part – that he whose love created
me will "one day" be like a gray and twisted
tree, and then a statue, as I was
before I woke. My Goddess –
can such cruelty be true?
Is Time, then, a greater God than all,
a savage God, such as the Titans were? Time,
I will defy you! My Lord and I will pray to Her

to change us both – a marble man, a wife of ivory
once more – and keep us in her temple, deathless,
beautiful, to teach the people faith-
fulness forever. I see –
yes, I can see that picture
in my mind! Oh, but my baby! Who
would take care of you? Wait – I mistake myself
again....a statue can't give birth, and my husband prays

now only that we may have a healthy child. And when
you've come, I must feed you, wash you, sing to you –
I must be your mother! Oh, too late
now! I, whose only mother
is a man, must learn
by "next year" how to raise a daughter!
For you are a girl, I know it. I can see
you in my mind – my effigy, fair as the Goddess

in her shrine, unchanged since the day your father made her.
So – that is how mortals triumph over Time!
The girl is her mother, but younger,
the boy his father's image
living on. I understand,
though he has not explained this to me.
The Goddess will make my next child be a boy!
And then.... but why does any woman have more than two

children? Some have two husbands, I've heard.... This is too hard.
I must not tire myself, he says, and I've thought
too much. But I have seen the pictures
in my mind — She is teaching
me how to live inside Time!
I've watched the mothers in the market,
bent above their babies — how they hold their hands
and help those fat little feet go stepping — left foot, right.

Victor Frankenstein: Howl, ye winds, and drive the tattered clouds
Like shadowy hell-hounds through the livid sky!
Hide in that veil, oh moon, your death-pale face!
For here, tonight, a terror shall transpire
surpassing any evil you have seen:
that cursed fiend approaches through the dark
to take the life of him who gave him life.

Because I would not make a female thing
as odious as he to be his mate,
he hunts me like a beast. Oh, how I thrill
with hatred and with fear! I seem to hear
his promise echoing from peak to peak:
"I will be with you on your wedding night."
But in my bosom, where my bride's sweet head

should rest, a pistol's ready to my hand.
As fate decides, in payment for my pride
I'll die, or else I'll live to rid the earth
of that foul scourge created by my hands.
Elizabeth awaits, and all the bliss
of consummated love – but I must watch
Until the dreadful climax is behind.

Elizabeth: Married at last, and he's out there declaiming
his tiresome emotions to the moon!
How sick I am of feelings—he stirs up
each last scrap from the bottom of the pot!
Let him pace and prattle all night long—
I will put perfume here, and here and...here
and wait at the window for the One who comes.

       The Monster: Ah, I see the hall that holds the Bride!
       She lights it like a lamp within the dark
       that mocks me for the darkness in my soul.
       Is that my foe who lurks there by her door?
       Conceited fool! He thinks I seek his life.
       He lacks the imagination to divine
       'Tis she, Elizabeth, I hunt this night.

Victor: Elizabeth! My angel, innocent
as dawn! So like my mother, whom you loved
as if she were your own! This one night past,
and your sweet body (how unlike that botch
that stalks me now) shall join with mine and make
another life! Oh, bliss to think of it –
Creation blessed by nature and by God!

If only I could tell her how I've suffered!
Elizabeth, my sister-bride, my toy,
my first invention! But I cannot pour
such vile pollution into her stainless soul.
Alone – alone! – I must confront my foe
to his or my undoing! Oh, ye gods –
No one has ever felt such pain as I!

Elizabeth: I hated them, his mother most of all,
who took me from the sun of Italy
to her cold, grey house and gave me to that fiend.
"A pretty present for you!" A girl of four,
given to a spoiled boy of five!
How he tormented me! Just pain at first,
later, those nasty things he said weren't sin

since we weren't siblings. And since they made
him feel such grand emotions — such mastery, such fear!
He made me a monster of hypocrisy
and all the household helped. I was their star,
their bird, their angel. I was so alone!
I feared that long pretense had made me sweet
and weak in truth. That was before He came.

    The Monster: She is an angel! When I told her how I'd suffered —
    how he tore my half-completed mate
    apart before my eyes — she pitied me.
    Before I found her, I was so alone!
    "First make me happy," I said to that base man,
    "and then I will be good." I would obey,
    as faithful as a dog, One who was kind to me.

    And she was kind. Obeying her, I killed
    the little boy, the pretty servant girl,
    the villain's friend — all the new favorites
    who would usurp her in the family's hearts.
    In all the world, she is the One who knows
    the innocence that budded in my soul,
    the goodness men have trampled and destroyed.

Victor: I feel him come! Oh, let my hand not shake,
and I will be Adam in a world new-made,
my sin redeemed, my own Eve in my arms!

> *Elizabeth:* The monster! He dreams of eiderdowns and babies
> and grandchildren upon his creaking knees!
> Shall I be a mother — I, this broken doll?

> > *Monster:* Shall each man find a wife to warm his bosom,
> > And each beast find a mate, and I alone
> > remain alone? No — he shall share my fate!

Victor: But if I fail, he will destroy us both
and roam the earth, to murder all mankind.
What bloody howlings then, what hellish scenes!

> *Elizabeth:* I feel him come! I feel his craving now!
> He thinks of death, but he will learn from me
> a better way to feed that appetite.

> > *Monster:* I will tear her loveliness apart,
> > her limbs that so reproach my loathsome form.
> > His hands will never mold those pliant curves!

Victor: Shriek, winds! Hide, moon! Come fiend! And let us try
that hideous strength against your creator's will!
The fate of all the world is in my hands!

> *Elizabeth:* He will obey! He'll kill once more for me,
> and then transport me to those sunny hills
> and serve me faithfully until we die.

Monster: Her loveliness...her limbs...those
pliant curves...

Victor: Tumultuous pain! Fell wrath! Exquisite dread!

Monster: Elizabeth, I come!

Elizabeth: Ah, Italy!

3

ELEUSIS

We know little of this part of the Mysteries, as the ancient sources tell us only that it consisted of "things enacted," probably a sacred pageant telling the tale of Demeter and Persephone, "things said," probably a series of brief liturgical or invocational statements, and "things shown," probably the Hiera and other objects, though again, we cannot be certain.

— Peter T. Struck, *The Eleusinian Mysteries*

1. Things Enacted

PROCESSION

Demeter, lady of the golden sword and glorious fruits. . . went to the towns and rich fields of men, disguising her form as an old woman. When she came to Eleusis, she sat near the wayside by the Maiden Well in a shady place over which grew an olive tree.

— *Homeric Hymn to Demeter*

She's ninety-two, wizened and bent as the witch in a fairy tale.
We thought she'd just keep shrinking, stamp on the ground and vanish, or drift
off on a foggy tide. But no – here's pancreatic cancer come to slay her.

Four weeks to go, maybe six. So I took flight from work and winter
to stay nine days in the land of glorious fruits, on the beach,
in a shady retirement place among olive trees. *The Mysteries*

*were held over nine days, heralded by messengers who proclaimed
a holy truce.* It isn't age that's tamed her, but some new potion
she takes daily to drive out her Furies. It almost disguises her

as someone else's mother, sets me searching for clues to know her by.
Tonight, for a treat, we're in the dining room, eating with folks
who'll still be here come spring. Like the mills of the gods, she grinds slow,

chews fine, and turns out surprises – I watch as she puts away salad,
tacos with salsa, green beans, corn soufflé, fudge cake, and coffee.
"Oh, Death, where is thy sting?" she used to say. She thought it was a prayer,

like "God deliver us!" Now I have to wonder – are the rumors
of her demise mistaken? The doctors don't know that greed of hers,
that gusto, so hard for the rest of us to live with. *On this day*

they keep a partial or complete fast. Every few bites I remember –
if the prognosis is correct, this is our last supper. The walls fall;
I clutch my chair arms until I can smile again. She tells me to stop playing

with my food. Too soon, it's night outside, and face it – dinner's done.
One task is left me. Not to wash the dishes, that comforting old chore,
but to get her back in the wheelchair and take her up to bed.

Sixty years since I was the baby in the buggy and she was a knock-out,
a pin-up girl in shorts and halter, dark hair caught back in two bows.
But still, the nurse calls her "pretty lady," the widowers smile

as I push her past. The doors open up before us like magic,
unfolding to the ancient night and the breath of dragons.
But if you have tasted food, you must go back again, beneath

the secret places of the earth. I want my Mommy. But she's no help now,
she can't keep in mind that she's dying. *What the gods send, we mortals bear
perforce.* I must be grown up enough to do this – put her to bed

and kiss her good-night for good. At dawn, the van to the airport,
and a continent will unroll itself between us. It's not likely
that I'll make the trip again. *A pair of goddesses, draped in a veil,*

are led with great pomp down to the sea. We pause on the terrace
to look at the Pacific. Wine-dark and silver rimmed, it pours itself out
on the sand, and falls back murmuring secrets. "I've never seen the sea,"

says an old poem I've been reading to her. But after all those decades
spent among cornfields and prairies, she *has* seen the sea, smelled the salt mist,
ambled the kelp-strewn beach, lived a half-lifetime reckoned by its tides.

She says, "I can't wait for summer. The ocean holds you right up
when you're swimming." *And of the birds of omen none came with true news for her.*
She's still chewing the olive she took from the table as we left.

The night assails me with its spell: the stars, the mild air, the scent
of blossoms. I want to weep. I think of another line she loves, "I will arise
and go now…"

        She says, "This olive is delicious. It's the black kind,
        from Greece. They're definitely better."

CHANT AND DANCE

So did they then, with hearts at one, greatly cheer each the other's soul and spirit, their hearts had relief from their griefs while each took and gave back joyousness.

— *Homeric Hymn to Demeter*

Back in her own room in Assisted Living,
she's in the armchair, I'm in the captain's chair
Daddy refinished fifty years ago. I read to her,
our ritual, and learn what I first learned
leaning back against her, the book open on my lap.

This book, *Silver Pennies.* She read it to my sister,
my brother, then me. One corner is dog-gnawed,
by Tarbaby, maybe, or Judge. The spine's been sutured
with a strip of adhesive tape crayoned orange
by somebody, maybe me.

Leaning back against her, between her arms,
I felt her voice in her chest before the words came warm
and dancing on her breath. Leaning there, I learned
that warmth was love. That rhythms breathed.
That language danced.

I read:
Before she has her floor swept
Or her dishes done,
Any day you'll find her
A-sunning in the sun!

She walks up the walk
Like a woman in a dream,
She forgets she borrowed butter
And pays you back cream!

I think: She longed to be the lazy neighbor in the poem. She had the charm, but not the same charmed life.

She says, "Why don't they give us more olives? I think those boys in the kitchen steal them!"

Dreaming of a prince,
Cinderella sat among the ashes long ago;
Dreaming of a prince,
She scoured the pots and kettles till they shone; and so,
After all and after all,
Gaily at the castle ball
Cinderella met her prince long and long ago.

She never met her prince; she had to marry someone else, and scour pots. "It ruined everything," she said.

"They always give us the green kind. I'd rather eat a piece of moldy cheese!"

Nymph, nymph, what are your beads?
     Green glass, goblin. Why do you stare at them?
Give them me.
          No.

Then I will howl all night in the reeds,
Lie in the mud and howl for them. . . .
Give me your beads, I desire them.
          No.

My first sex education. The power of beauty. The power of refusal.

>"If only they'd give us the *good* kind, the
>ones from Greece."

I will arise and go now, and go to Innisfree,
And a small cabin build there, of clay and wattles made;
Nine bean rows will I have there, a hive for the honey bee,
And live alone in the bee-loud glade.

>I see her reciting, hands in the sink, eyes
>out the window. There is another realm.
>To be discontented is a gift.

>>"But back to olives: I can't remember
>>the last time I had a decent one."

As soon as the fire burns red and low,
And the house upstairs is still,
She sings me a queer little sleepy song,
Of sheep that go over a hill.

And one slips over and one comes next,
And one runs after behind,
The grey one's nose to the white one's tail,
The top of the hill they find..

>Every night she tries to join me
>in the dance, to recite the tricky,
>shifting repetitions.

"Now, wait — the white one's nose —
Why are they running uphill,
anyway?"

And one slips over and one comes next,
The good little, grey little sheep!

And I watch as the fire burns red and low,
And she says that I fall asleep.

"And I watch as the fire burns red and low,
And she says that I fall asleep."

2. Things Revealed

INITIATION

The poetry is over — time, as she used to say, for B-E-D.
And she'd raise one eyebrow, enacting the Terrible Mother.
Now, between the chanting and the phoned words that will fly
through the fruitless air until the day Atropos cuts her thread,
I must continue the reversal, mother her, and put her to bed.
I help her remove her blouse and bra. Her skin is very white, a sign

of great beauty. Her breasts astound me — round as melons,
they rest at her waist, hung from long wrinkly streamers.
How I hated, in junior high, that unseemly Gospel verse,
read right out in church, "Blessed are the paps that thou hast sucked."
Pity stops my fingers, then terror moves them to quickly button up
her pajama top. I slide her slacks down from her waist. Her belly,

once an heap of wheat, is now a slack purse emptied of its treasure.
Beneath it, draped in a Depends, is the most holy and mysterious region,
entered only by the Priest. I ask if she needs to make a last trip
to the bathroom. "No," she says, "I'm too tired; I'll take the chance."
And so I'm spared that final revelation. But my hands still tremble
as the slacks slide to her feet and I hold her arm (a stick, an olive branch)

while she steps free. Her thigh bones are sharp as blades; the flesh,
as if wanting no more to do with her, hangs loose in drooping flags.
Soon she'll be down to the essential image, the one that's frightened us
forever. Not the crepe and pasteboard *danse macabre*, but her real bones —
femurs, tibia, tarsals. Not the trite icon on the pirate flag,
but her real skull, the one she used to butt her way out of her mother.

Bone of my bone. She's grown into a Sybil: these bones prophesy,
tell me that I must die. This month I complete my sixtieth year.
Helped by no goddess's spell, I am two-in-one, mourning child
disguised as an old woman. Initiate, frightened and free,
I take from her hand this clue, this thread that leads to the end.
I help Mother onto the bed, hold her in a hug that must last out

both our lives. "Oh, that's good!" she says. Then she complains: the mattress
is all wrong, it has ridges. "No rest for the wicked." If I had a dime
for every time she's said that, I'd have a lot of dimes. I remind her:
her own bed will be moved to this room next week. "So they say,
but I'm not holding my breath. Oh, well. I don't suppose anybody
ever died of a lumpy bed." She lies back, sighs, and, pleased after all,

announces, "Good-bye, world." Eyes closed, she's an instant effigy.
Not an eyelid-twitch. I bend down to make sure she's breathing.
She is Eleanor on her tomb, Nefertiti bound in spices,
Elaine the Lily Maid on the river, her nose a lovely prow.
She's going on, regardless. The rest of the ritual's up to me.
I kiss her cheek; it feels like cobweb. Then I find there are words

I can intone, the old devotions. "I love you." Her lips move,
"I love you, too." That seems to cover it. But at the door
I turn back and do it all again, a magic against ending.
Another kiss, "I love you." She says, "Thank you. For everything."
The child, you'd think, would be the one to say that, but I don't.
I turn out the light and leave.

I'm on the terrace, in the blessed dark.
The sea is still pacing up and down the beach, pouring out its old oblation.
Salt wets my face; I taste it. The air smells of olive blossoms.
I breathe it in hard, it pours out rough. I breathe it in. *Happy is she
who, having seen these rites, goes below the hollow earth;
for she knows the end of life and she knows its god-sent beginning.*

3. Things Said

OBITUARY

Task

No black-edged stationery these days – just a form
to fill out on the Web site of the *North County News*.
Education and employment. Church and club affiliations.
Other major public contributions, hobbies, and/or interests.

> No place to write: "Just before I fall asleep, it hits me,
> *My mother's dead*." The bed lurches, the earth itself gives way.
> But then, awake, I'm all grown up again. And she was ninety-two,
> and hated it when children made a fuss. So I sleep to please her.

No place, either, to put down a grade or ranking, e.g.
"An interesting person, if only she weren't your mother."
(When I was ten, she said she pictured her soul as the soft,
elastic, colorless inside of a jelly bean. I thought mine

> was more like the Washington Monument: I didn't say that,
> but saw, for the first time, that I would outlast her.)
> No one did less in a long lifetime to make an impression
> in these online boxes. No one would have hated the form more.

She who walked through the yards of neighbors she hadn't met
(because that was the shortest route to the stores) would scorn
my pious research, my typing and deleting. "Don't be a half-wit,"
she'd say. "Just write down some stuff and stop making such a fuss."

Thirteen Facts

She was always the prettiest and smartest girl in her class. We know this on her own authority.

She dropped out of college and got married upon becoming pregnant in her freshman year. It was August, 1929.

She often said, to her children and others, that she was never in love with her husband.

On fall Saturdays, she made my big sister stay home and clean the house instead of attending high school football games.

All her life, she recited poems she'd memorized in high school. For instance,

> *But oh! that deep romantic chasm which slanted*
> *Down the green hill athwart a cedarn cover!*
> *A savage place! as holy and enchanted*
> *As e'er beneath a waning moon was haunted*
> *By woman wailing for her demon-lover!*

When I was growing up, she had crushes on Jerry Lewis, Leonardo da Vinci, the rector of our church, and each of my boyfriends in turn.

She owned, and played devotedly, 78 RPM records of five classical pieces: Brahms' *Hungarian Rhapsody*, Khachaturian's *Saber Dance*, the *Hallelujah Chorus*, the *Triumphal March* from *Aida*, and Marian Anderson singing "Panis Angelicus."

Once the mailman rang while she was scrubbing the kitchen floor. She rose from her knees, rag in hand, and greeted him with, "Don't ever get married!"

She could stick a Salerno butter cookie on the end of her nose.

When I told her I had been named high school Valedictorian, she thought I was lying.

She underwent electro-shock therapy three times between 1949 and 1982.

She was a widow for twenty years.

She was still wearing eye liner the week she died.

Dislikes

Buttoning up her high-button shoes. Having to get to school on time. Darning stockings. Beating rugs. Getting chilblains. Norma Shearer. Laurel and Hardy. Boring textbooks. Rules. Rationing. Bad coffee. Sudden loud noises. Scrubbing floors. Ironing. Show-offs and conceited people. Boring people. Narrow-minded people. Stupid people. Vulgar people. Cheap people. Women who were sissies. Women who were bossy. Know-it-all doctors. Mayor Daley. Dean Martin. Billy Graham. The New York Yankees. Bad television. Artificial Christmas trees. Store-bought bread with no backbone. Washing windows. Cooking. Forks with the wrong kind of tines. Cups with the wrong kind of handles. Plates that were too heavy. Adlai Stevenson. Arthur Godfrey. Ugly buildings. Spoiled children. Being too hot or too cold. Missing her nap. Houses where fields used to be. Smog on the Sierra Nevadas. Plastic on the beach. Paul Harvey, Richard Nixon, Gore Vidal. People with no opinions.

Worries

That she'd never be as pretty as her sister. That we'd never have enough money. That the sofa upholstery would wear out if she didn't keep a plastic cover on it. That people would find out her first baby wasn't really premature. That her house would never be as nice as her sister's. That her children would be conceited. That her son would turn out to be a sissy. That I would never get married. That I would get married and not live at home after college. That it would rain on my wedding day. That my father didn't impress the men he worked for. That a thief would find the heirloom silver she hid in a Kotex box. That she'd have to give a book review at Book Club. That the neighbors would see we'd put the milk bottle on the kitchen table instead of using a pitcher. That her clothes weren't fancy enough. That her sons-in-law wouldn't find her attractive. That she'd never really be in love. That people would find out she'd been in a mental hospital. That her daughters would betray her by getting married before they got pregnant.

Sayings

It must be jelly 'cause jam don't shake like that. Straighten up and fly right. Buy it before the hoarders get it. Put your little heady down. I worked like a nigger. Were you born in a barn? You're getting too big for your britches. Life is no bed of roses. Peel me a grape! You wouldn't say "shit" if you had a mouthful. Isn't that the limit? Night brings the bums home. If I've told you once, I've told you a thousand times. You look like a refugee. What's gotten into you? As easy as falling off a log. As much as you could stick in your eye. I was tickled pink. You could have knocked me over with a feather. I'm putting my foot down. Lend me your nightcap and sing me a soothing lullaby. You and I are going to go to the mat. You slay me. Like nobody's business. Strictly from hunger. Hell's bells! The damnedest thing. You need a good, swift kick. I'd give my eye teeth for that. Don't make me laugh! Enough is too much. I'm beside myself. I'm at the end of my rope. Can you imagine?

Education: Davina was always the prettiest and the smartest girl in her class. Boys who were in love with her included Billy, Fred, Wallace, Eddie, Sam, and Johnny. Her mother taught her that a lady never leaves the house without her hat and gloves. Also the secrets of how to darn a sock, make a soufflé, rinse her hair with vinegar, start seeds in a cold frame, and tell the robin's song from the cardinal's. Her father taught her to swim and to ride a bike. She walked through the woods to dancing lessons. When she was old, she learned to love California and Mexicans, who have richer souls. She read every day of her life and became a Democrat before it was too late.

Marriage: She got married too soon, and they didn't have enough money to stick in your eye. Her husband loved her like mad; he was no slouch in the romance department. A good father, and handy around the house. But too nice for his own damn good. The one time he showed some spunk was making her move out to California after they'd lived in Illinois all their lives, and then he died too soon. Hell's bells — their souls didn't match. He never cared if they were rich or poor. And he didn't enjoy a good argument the way Davina did. Maybe that was the secret.

Employment: She was a typist right after they got married, and took the train into Chicago just like a man. But she was morning sick and had to throw up on the tracks in Union Station, so that was that. Davina had dinner on the table by 5:15 every goddamn night for forty years. Scrubbed the linoleum, hung laundry outside on a line, grew beans and tomatoes and canned them until frozen vegetables came along. They were never rich: she didn't have a cleaning lady until she was almost fifty, and then it was too late. Secretly, she loved hanging out the laundry. And doing the garden — that was good for her soul.

Children: Three, a lovely son with blond curls and two girls who were pretty enough and never any trouble. He had a perfect nose when he was little, and then when he got to high school it looked like it had been broken, and he never even played football! He has a PhD and got a medal for Distinguished Civilian Service from the Secretary of Defense. Davina never let the kids get too big for their britches: they had to do their chores and put their shoulders to the wheel. Gave them the riches of books and nature's secrets. Didn't bury their souls in store-bought junk or let them grow up too soon. Laughed with them. Made them think.

Accomplishments: Brought up three children (see above) who turned out fine, though none of them is what you'd call rich. Had to fight men off with a stick. (That photographer in Florida thought Davina was the prettiest woman he'd ever seen, poor soul.) Stayed married for fifty-one years, although she never was in love with her husband. Moved and redecorated fifteen times. Had a green thumb. Called a spade a spade. Kept driving to Indiana for the grandkids when their father died too soon. Once doubled and re-doubled in a bridge game and won. Made people laugh. Kept up her appearance and never spent a cent on clothes.

Other major public contributions, hobbies, and/or interests: Had a Victory Garden. Helped out at the nursery school until that little snip in charge said Davina acted like a child herself. Belonged to AAUW, and kept the secret that she didn't graduate from college. Went to Episcopal, Congregational, and Presbyterian churches, and to the Mission with her Mexican friends. (Couldn't believe that stuff, though, not to save her soul: her parents never took her to Sunday school, so maybe it was too late.) Joined the D.A.R. when she was too old to go to meetings. Wasn't rich, but wrote checks to the Sierra Club and Public Television. Walked on the beach and talked to surfers. Kept the yard man at Casa Del Sol from ruining the big willow with his goddamn shears.

Preceded in death by: Grandpa Waterman, who fought in the Battle of Antietam. Rich Grandpa Gene and Grandma Elsie. Mama. Papa, who loved Davina the best. Mr. Peterson at the corner store. Lovey, Whiskers, Tarbaby, Judge, and Max. Uncle Ernie, Uncle Will, Aunt Alice, Aunt Anna, Aunt Rose. Her husband Johnny. Her brother Graham, her sisters Anita and Kathleen. Cousin Janet, Cousin Pearl, Cousin Corinne. Her son-in-law, Kenny. Johnny's five sisters and their husbands. Grandsons Stephen and John. Lillian Gish, Rudolph Valentino, Rudy Vallee. Gracie Burns. Poor little Marilyn Monroe. Amelia Earhart, Albert Einstein, Albert Schweitzer. Eleanor Roosevelt, Mamie Eisenhower. All those Kennedys who died too soon. Walt Kelly and Al Capp. Gertrude, Milly and George in Assisted Living. Ephra and Tom downstairs, God rest their souls. The photographer in Florida. Whoever sent those secret admirer cards. Billy. Fred. Wallace. Eddie. Sam.

LAST WORDS

And she was like an ancient woman who is cut off from childbearing and the gifts of garland-loving Aphrodite, like the nurses of king's children who deal justice, or like the housekeepers in their echoing halls.

— Homeric Hymn to Demeter

After the Turner Classics movie, I call her, Boston to southern California.
For the first time, a strange voice answers, a nurse has to hand her the phone:
"It's your daughter, Sarah." And Mother says, "From the East," as if greeting
a Wise Man. She sounds horizontal, drugged. She knows me, but still doesn't know
that she's dying. (*Hideous to keep reminding her — news of nothingness*

falling into nothingness, fished out again to gleam for half an hour,
then sink back below the surface.) So I only say, "You sound really tired."
"I've just had a baby," she declares. "I bet you're wondering how I got it."
Her triumph cuts through the drug-haze: she's 92 and still the cat's meow!
I know she does have a baby — a lost doll that lay around the residence

until she adopted it. She sings to it, dresses it in gown and booties,
ties on its bonnet. She was a dab hand at babies, and now the youngest
is sixty and lives in the East. (*Once Santa brought my baby doll a jacket, pink*
plaid flannel. When, in May, I found a piece of the same fabric in a drawer,
Mother explained: Mrs. Santa sent some extra cloth in case the baby

needed a new jacket.) "Well, well," I say. I can't bring out the questions
she's expecting: Boy or girl? What's its name? Who's the father? And *how*
did they manage sex in Assisted Living? Instead I talk about my own
grown-up baby. "Lisa was here this afternoon. We ate ice cream
and watched the final episode of 'Xena: Warrior Princess.'" Mother

may know nothing of Xena, but I'm sure she'll like that "Warrior."
"Oh, and she's fine?" she asks, meaning Lisa. Sometimes she confuses
the two of us, daughter and granddaughter, or blends us into one small,
dark-haired, over-educated girl. I take this as an unwitting compliment.
"Yes, very fine," I say, "She's married, now, you know." I report

on their happiness, their condo, their jobs. Then what to say?
"Did you get the poem I sent you?" "Oh, *yes*, it was *won*derful."
"Did you like the part about the fish in Grandma's pond?"
I want to say, but that would ask too much – she won't remember it,
and she's not up to the talking. She who sang "Bye Baby Bunting"

so I'd know that words could play is almost at the end of words. (*I wrote
a book of poems, and she said, "It makes my whole life whole and perfect."
Unsettling, because she never praised me. Surprising, too – I thought
the poems were about my own life.*) Silence. How can I keep up
this one-way chatter, bereft of her gossip and complaints, her annoying

interruptions? "I bought a hat today!" I describe it—pale straw, with pale
pink stripes and a bunch of poppies on the band, shading from pink to orange.
(*I was little… a picnic lunch out in a meadow… she flattened the tall,
pale grass and made a nest for me to sit in.*) "But I wonder if I'll ever
wear it – spring just won't come. The snow's still three feet deep.

The bird feeder was empty for a month – I couldn't get to it. Finally, today,
I climbed over the porch railing and edged along where there's bare earth
beneath the eaves and took it down." (*She taught me bird names, whistled me
their songs. I learned some of her lore, but always thought that someday I'd know
all the names – birds, flowers, constellations – just by becoming a woman,*

like my mother. Know-it-alls run in our female line. Take the time she sat chatting with my baby on her lap and told me she looked forward to being dead, because then you know everything. I said, "Maybe after you're dead you're just dead." She considered that notion and told me I was wrong.) "On the way back with the feeder," I say, "I had an idea – I walked right on top of the snow!"

"Oh, *did* you?" The kind of thing she lived for – a small miracle in the midst of daily chores. "Mom, I'd better hang up. It's after eleven here, and I'm meeting a friend for coffee in the morning." "Well, be careful. We'll worry if you do anything wild." I laugh and promise to be careful. "Good-bye. I love you." "I love you, too." Next day, after the coffee date,

the phone rings: she died during the night. "I told her I'd bought a hat!" I tell my sister, and we laugh. We plan a family gathering to plant her ashes next to our father's plot, a time to tell Mother Stories to all the cousins.
                               Oh, Mother, you could tell
a funny story. You'd say it was the talk of my new hat that killed you,

and you sure surprised Dr. Babyface Smarty-Pants, who thought you had a couple weeks left. I want to call California and say, "Don't worry, Mom, I do wild things all the time. I tell the truth. I write poems. I make people laugh. I had a baby who grew up a Warrior Princess. I know everything, and I owe it all to you. I did what you did: the opposite of anything you told me."

And when this had been said, the goddess changed her stature and her looks,
thrusting old age away from her: beauty spread round about her
*   and sweetness wafted from her robes. From her divine body a light shone afar,*
so that the strong house was filled with brightness as with lightning.
And so she went out from the palace.

4

LATE DAY

DOWN IN THE DARK

After three days of equinoctial
rain, I fall asleep to sounds of geese
leaving and dream right back to nineteen

forty-nine, the old house on Ashland
Avenue, the basement. The windows,
high above my head, are filled with snow.

The furnace is humming a grumbly
song, leaking a square of firelight
around its iron door. At the dim

edge of the light-bulb's circle, Mason
jars gleam in rows – tomatoes, onions,
peas, beans, cauliflower, peaches. Bright

as the Christmas balls boxed and waiting
in the attic, each jar sits wax-sealed
and dreaming, remembering sun, roots,

rain. They make me think of my mother,
bending over her hoe, then over
the steaming stove, boiling down summer

to keep us all going in the cold.
Outside, each puddle or pond is sealed
with ice. But down here, behind the lines

of laundry dried by the furnace's
secret sun, I find two round wooden
tubs where wintering goldfish swim. Orange,

tomato-red, peach, white, and pinto,
they flick and weave within the glassy
water. These fish live in my Grandma's

basement, not ours. But this is a dream,
and I kneel by the tubs and watch fish
go round and round, dreaming of their rock-

lined pool, the roof of water lilies,
the dragonflies dipping to their kiss.
I'm six. I know that fish are cold clear

through, but I have a furnace inside.
It throbs like the big one, that engine
hauling the house toward Christmas. Then

comes my birthday, then Valentine's Day
and Easter. Then summer — bare feet, hide
and seek, peaches, tomatoes, and gold-

fish in Grandma's pool. I'll be seven
and half then. I see, for the first
time, that I have a brain that can think

all this and still be here in winter,
in the basement. I can keep it down
inside me, like secrets. I can hear

autumn rain, half-waking, and still see
the high, snow-filled windows, the bright jars,
the laundry, the furnace, the fish...

WHO WAS THAT MASKED MAN?

For years, in front of those black-and-white TV's, we believed
we'd grow up to be cowboys. Boys, girls, not one of us escaped
the dream – the drop to horseback from the balcony, the ride
through the dust to catch the black hat, the umpteenth daring rescue
of somebody helpless and blonde. Oh, it was fun to be the good
guy, it was easy. All it took was a white hat, a pair of six-guns,

and a strong, good-natured horse. The bad guys had their own guns,
of course, but were handicapped by being stupid and so unbelievably
bad that we knew they had to lose, or what was the point of goodness?
Every day we sat on the floor and watched them, after we'd made our escape
from school – Roy Rogers, Hopalong, the Lone Ranger galloped to the rescue
while our fathers, wearing hats, were heading home for dinner, riding

in trains and car pools. How we wished for silver stallions to ride
instead of our beat-up Schwinns! Like cowboys tied to chairs with our guns
out of reach on the table, we were stuck in the unrescuable
state of childhood, bound by homework and chores. We believed
we could master the thousand ways they taught us to escape –
the candle flame, the broken glass, the signal flashed to the good

Indian hiding outside the cabin. No girl dreamed of being that goody-
goody sidekick, Dale Evans. We would twirl lariats, wear chaps, and ride
after bad guys every day. Sometimes we would even help Roy escape
from the abandoned mine, bind up his wounds with one hand and gun
down desperadoes with the other. In light of this, it was hard to believe
that our mothers could tell us to get up and set the table, or run to rescue

the backyard laundry from the rain. But Mom was the Law. To rescue
our dignity, we obeyed, muttering that we would run away for good
and live on a ranch if only we could get the train conductors to believe
that we were older. Now we *are* older — and not one of us is riding
down bad guys through the dust. Where are our trusty horses? Our guns?
Our bunk beds on the ranch? A weekend in Vermont is our "escape,"

and our children, watching medics holler "clear!" and gangsters escaping
with their semi-automatics, would laugh at our dreams of rescue —
those leaps to horseback, those bloodless chases, those miniature six-guns.
They know it's not easy as black and white to tell the bad from the good,
and that when you're tied up with the fuse burning, you can forget about riding
back to the Bar-B Ranch beside the blonde. Yet somehow, we secretly believe

that we're too good to end up losing. Before the sun sets, one more beyond-belief
rescue! There are a thousand ways — the fuse fizzles, the bad guy drops the gun,
the sidekick escapes, and listen! — from over the hill, the cavalry comes riding!

NOTES ON A MS. FOUND IN A GAZEBO

for Peggy Miller

1. *Under Lenten rain's lash, forsythias flail, buds ache and burst.*

The poet suggests that spring is a time of painful labor
and recalls Christ's flogging.   See T. S. Eliot, *The Wasteland.*

2. *My heart feels – and my sweating, driven limbs – the guerdon promised:*
   the Guest who comes with color, savor, odor heaped in her hands.

Salvation by works: if she does her spring chores diligently,
Summer – paradisiacal, personified – will visit her.

3. *Not I, but that Other, Better She perfects Her labors – leaves*
   raked, seeds started, annuals planted, mulch applied, flagstones scrubbed.

She imagines that her neighbor surpasses her in virtue.

4. *Again unready, I watch the expected Guest pass my door.*
   She sips iced tea with my Neighbor, deploring my undone chores.

Disgrace: she has failed to merit summer's full delight. The tale
of the Wise and Foolish Virgins is echoed here, as is
the Protestant work ethic of the poet's New England home.

5. *Age is my true guest. She brings her wisest sister, gray Despair.*

Spring's promise will never be fulfilled for her – she is too old
for that. She renounces the cycle of longing and letdown.

6. *Fevered, weak, good for nothing, I laze and lap up all her sweets.*
 I rest like Mary at the Savior's feet...

                                        The poet falls ill.
Unable to work, she indulges in seasonal pleasures.

7. *For my own eye's delight I strung the morning glory's blue,*
 set the white impatiens by the geranium's red and green.

She fancies that she herself is the Guest for whom she labored .

8. *I am the cat beneath the hedge – she toils not, and the sun-warmed*
 breeze brings her news of all the busy world.

                                        The idle poet,
after misapplying the Parable of the Lilies,
identifies with a creature renowned for its languidness.

9. *I am Elect, Beloved, Dryad, daughter of light and shade and moving leaf.*

She then carelessly combines terms from Calvinist doctrine
and the Song of Songs with reference to a pagan nature sprite.

10. *Mother, savior, summer...*

                        The manuscript breaks off here. The stains
on the paper appear to be made by strawberries and wine.

SIGHTINGS

To see them you must have faith, and time to wait
quietly. This summer, surgery
worked. You sit, sliced and stapled,
in the magnolia's shade, sit
where the feeder, like a thurible,
swings from its wire vine. And as you sit,

still as a maiden in a green-stitched grove
awaiting the holy unicorn,
still as a lady hermit
becalmed within her bower,
then you may be vouchsafed the whirring
of wings — alarming, sometimes, so close and out

of nowhere. Fear not! Breathe, and see how speed, verve,
elegance surprise your sheltered space
and shrink to a darting core:
a dark comma suspended
above the feeder, haloed by blur,
beak sunk deep to sip sweetness from plastic blooms.

It is gone. It is back again. In humming-
bird time, perhaps decades have elapsed
while you've drawn a single breath
or turned a page. And why not?
You have learned, lately, to put up with
these mysteries. Just keep the faith by the feeder:

be a virgin set out to decoy wonders,
or an ancient abbess training
to be patient as a saint.
Just wait for the whir, the blur,
the body bent like a crooked finger
beckoning from beyond. Keep a count, in case

you're asked to testify: tally the females,
undeniable in black and white,
the males dark from feet to beak
except for those moments – rare
as syzygy – when the late sun's rays
laser through leaves to light up the ruby throat.

CERTAIN MAPLES

don't wait. They rush
into reds while others
are keeping green, or yellowing
discreetly at the edges.

                         Sore thumbs,
throbbing where the road
curves past the fruit stand,
or worse, by your front curb,
they flare up,

                         garish as hookers.
They won't go quietly —
they burn on like heretics,
bent on it. They point
their flaming fingers, heap

                         coals of fire,
cumulus, higher
than houses. Even at night
they're at it, strident
in the dark, blaring their brassy alarms.

IN OCTOBER

the crows come yelling down.
They sift through branches like a loud
black crash and land in a thick litter

on the grass, glittering, dark and sharp
as scattered tacks. The crows come thicker
than the yellow leaves, as if the colored month

had cracked open to the back of things
and black crows streamed out of the crack —
Van Gogh's crows across the yellow wheat.

Just when the year is yellow-red and ripe,
the crows stalk our lawns in wicked,
hieroglyphic packs, jabbing and jerking

with their hard black beaks. They yell.
They wrap us in their bleak, barbed-wire cries.
Each day we wake to warnings: October's husk

will crack. Black winter's coming back.

LATE DAY

When the pond is still.
When trees are garnet and copper

and the air itself is gold.
When the far shore is doubled

on the water: wet paints
on paper folded, pressed, unfolded.

When you feel no wind,
but yellow birch leaves tremble.

When three mallards glide by, green heads
gleaming. When sound sleeps. When,

for an hour, there is nothing to wish for.
When the air cools and the water

darkens. When gray geese raise a ruckus,
saying you cannot stay.

NESTING DOLLS

A woman-shaped womb of wood,
the face a madonna icon, rounded.
The eyes are wide black circles,
the round, red mouth is sweet.
The cheeks are pink circles.
The face says, "I have a sweet,
round secret.' The belly swells,
blazoned with fat pink roses.

The woman inside her
has an eyebrow raised.
Her face is less round.
The cheeks are smaller;
the mouth is not a heart.
Her face says, "I am thinking."
Her belly wears one rose.

The woman inside her
has eyes that droop.
Her mouth is crowded
by her circle cheeks.
Her face says, "I have doubts."
Her belly hugs clenched buds.

The woman inside her
has tiny eyes, no cheeks.
The mouth is just a mark.
Her face says, "I'm afraid."
Her belly a bare twig.

Inside her: face of two
black dots, one red,
says "I don't know."
Belly two green spots.

Inside her, egg of wood,
Unbreakable. Says,
"I am here."

3:00 A.M.: QUESTIONING CASSIOPEIA

On burning soles, I cross the bedroom floor
and lay hot head against the freezing pane.
Above the pines, the queen in her sequined chair
sits cold and unperturbed, a sovereign

of ice. But she is burning in the moon-
less sky as I burn in this window shrine.
"Why must we watch all night, and burn alone
like signal fires on hilltops, when no sign

of danger can be seen?" I ask. "No child
cries out in fever or a dream, no pain
or worry keeps me from my sleep — no wild
beasts prowl my garden, no thief can gain

entry to this house, where all is well.
My husband snores at ease. Why then, am I
condemned and set ablaze?" "I cannot tell,"
the Queen replies, "but it is heresy

to question what's decreed by ancient rule.
It is our lot — we burn, and then we cool."

ON WINGAERSHEEK BEACH

She walks into the ocean, like a turtle
leaving eggs safe in sand, above tide-
line. But the cold shocks her legs
to a stop. Waves gnaw her shins and chew
the sand she stands on. They tug toward the smooth deeps

that breathe up and down without breaking. She leans
back, away from the ice-white daytime
moon. She is through with its ebbs
and flows now, won't dance to its tune. High
on the beach, behind her, her daughter lies side-

by-side with her tan young man. She has cramps, poor
girl; she won't go near the water, but
will turn each oiled surface
sunward and brown all day, a brochette
tenderized to his taste. The mother, meanwhile,

stands like a post in the shallows. Splashing kids
dash past her and toddlers stagger after
sanderlings. She sees nothing
that needs her — while the mothers of young
ones caw their anxiety like sea gull cries,

she is free to swim as she pleases. She stands,
still. She is afraid. The near future
holds a change she knows by heart —
the freezing plunge, the panicky, fast
strokes. And then the bliss, exhilaration, love

beyond measure of one's own warm core. The memory's clear, but she does not believe.
A year ago, the last time,
she was younger. Yelling kids can tease
the literal surf and dance in its teeth. She,

cursed with learning, is stuck in Shelley's ocean,
in Crane's, in the cruel sea of ballads,
flailing the sand with tattered
tragedies. Gulls call, "Beware! The waves
take heat and breath, change you, at best, to a fish,

or a seal on gray rocks, gray muzzle turned toward
shore, where your daughter will pace and cry."
"Nonsense," she answers, the turned
tide rising to knee, to thigh. She need
only decide, she decides. She doesn't move.

THE BLACK SEA

Once it was out of sight, that sea that can spill
like ink across the map of any country.
We'd heard of it, were told that all roads lead
by long or short ways to its dismal shore.
We had our doubts — it sounded like a myth —

but now there are days when we catch a tang of salt,
glimpse a black glitter from our bedroom window.
So, like a swimmer lowering a toe,
or Mithridates, who died on the Black Sea's shore,
I take each day, in my mind, a little dose —

inoculation against that bitter water.
As people do. A spoonful of dread gulped down
and then it's over — time to drive to work,
or read the paper or, sometimes, crack a joke —
prophylaxis to put panic in its place

and keep one's distance from the thought of death.
It haunted Mithridates, so brave in war,
so terrified at table. It haunts me —
I speak, my husband, of your death, not of mine.
For you, so different from that conqueror,

are drawn as he was to that same black sea.
Each day you must drink a small dose of its waters
not in your mind, as I do, but in your body,
that flesh I cherish as my oldest friend.
No prophylactic fantasies for you —

the poison pools, builds deltas day by day,
advances under cover every night.
Unnoticeable as the Black Sea's tides,
it rises always, claiming new colonies:
toes, kidneys, retinas, the mortal map

that limns your life and is the world to me.
In the end, it will ebb and float you on its flood
from shallows of pain back to the endless sea.
If I think of this each day in a small dose,
will it be antidote to suffering?

Not yours — I mean my own when, ankle deep,
I yield you to the tug of the dark waves
that pull you from me toward no farther shore.
Mithridates, at bay by the Black Sea,
drank hemlock without harm, his will betrayed

by his own stratagem. A loyal guard,
obedient, dispatched him with his sword.
If I think of that each day — the loyal guard
myself, and you the cornered king —
will I become immune? Will it help me live?

Author

Sarah Getty's first book of poems, *The Land of Milk and Honey*, was part of the James Dickey Contemporary Poetry Series (University of South Carolina Press, 1996).Her poem "That Woman" is included in *Birds in the Hand* (2004, Farrar, Straus, Giroux). Ms. Getty's fiction has appeared in *The Iowa Review* and in the anthology *Still Going Strong* (Haworth Press, 2005). She lives in Bedford, Massachusetts.